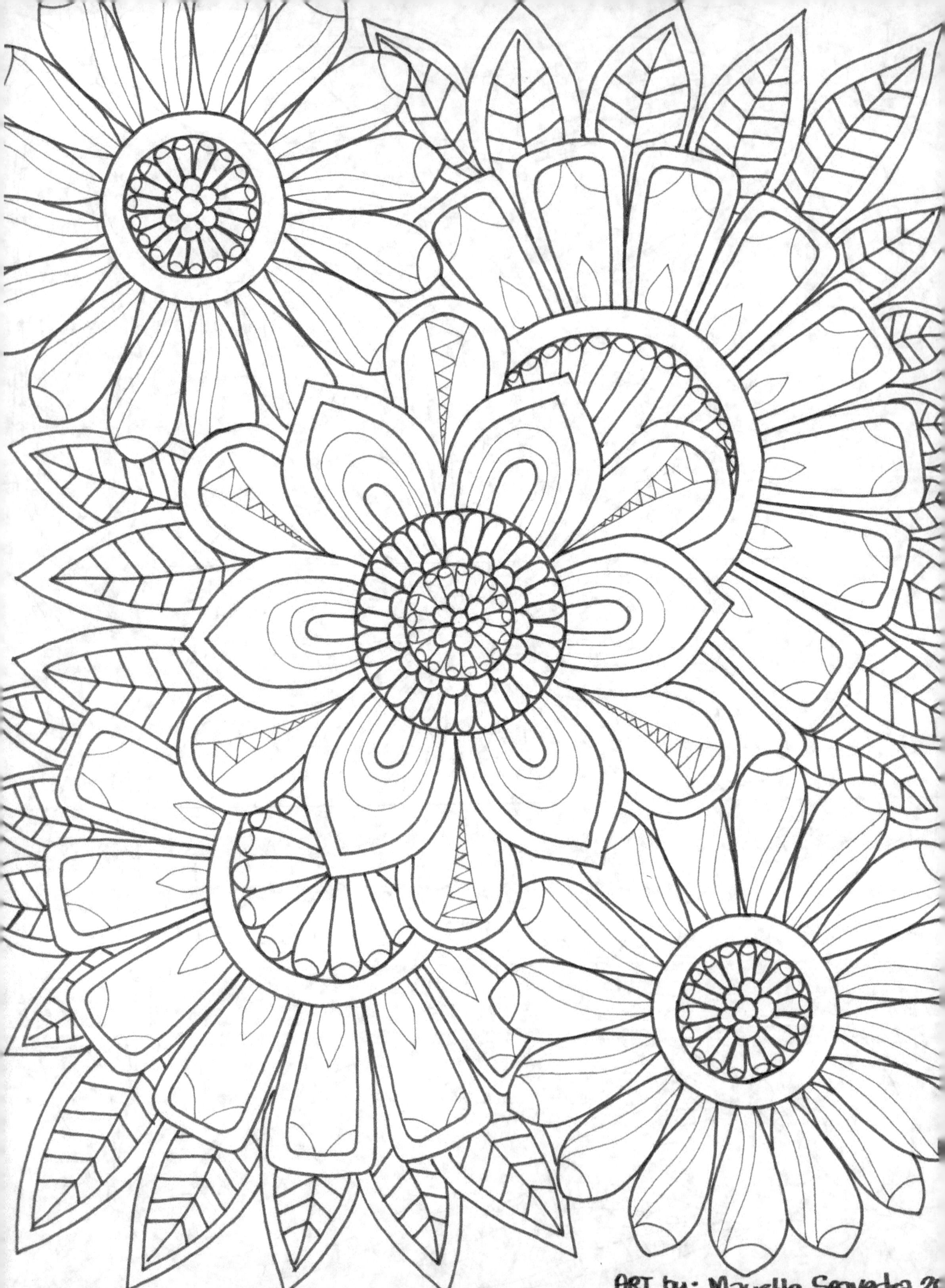

ART by: Mayette Saavedra 20

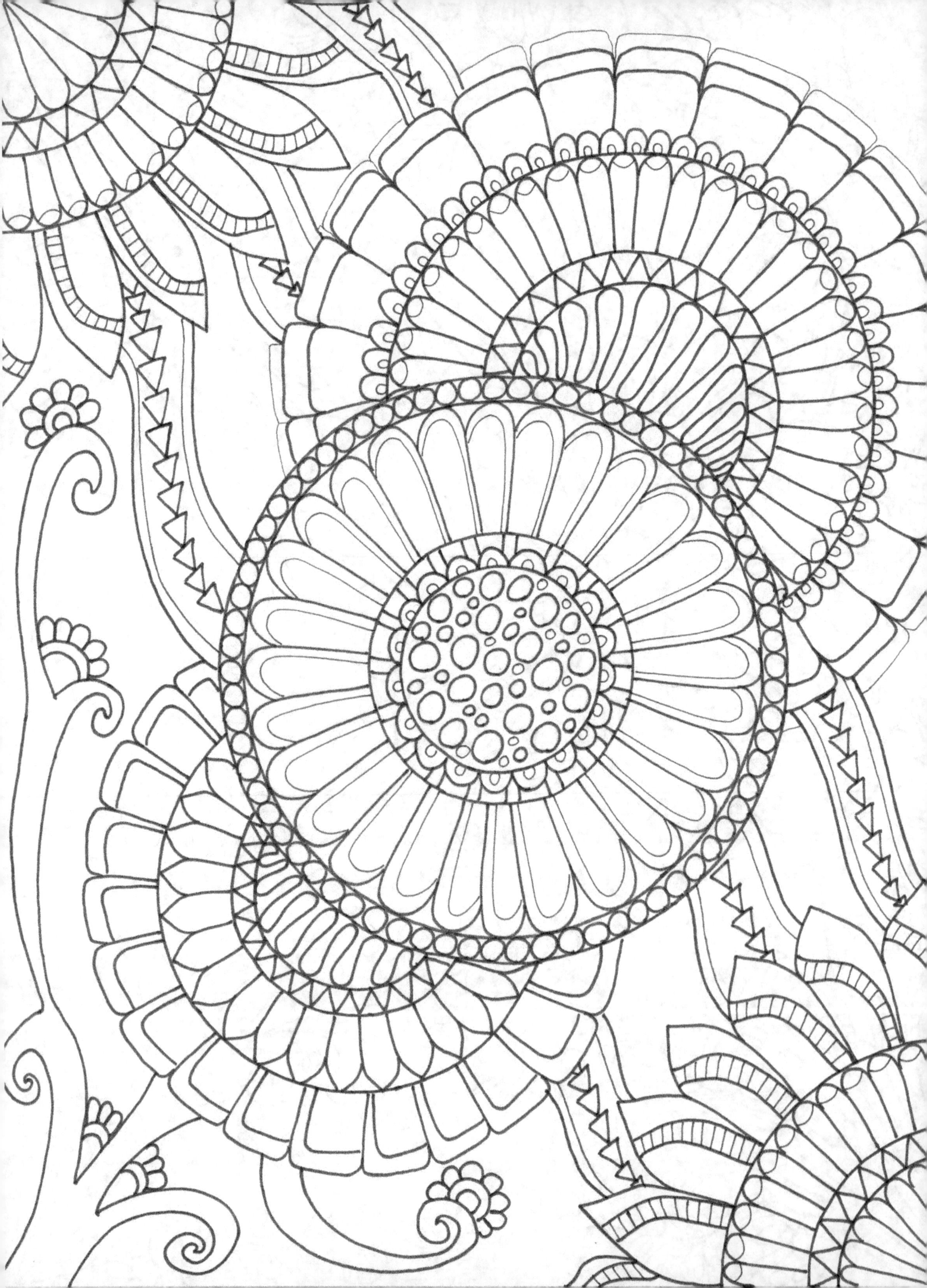

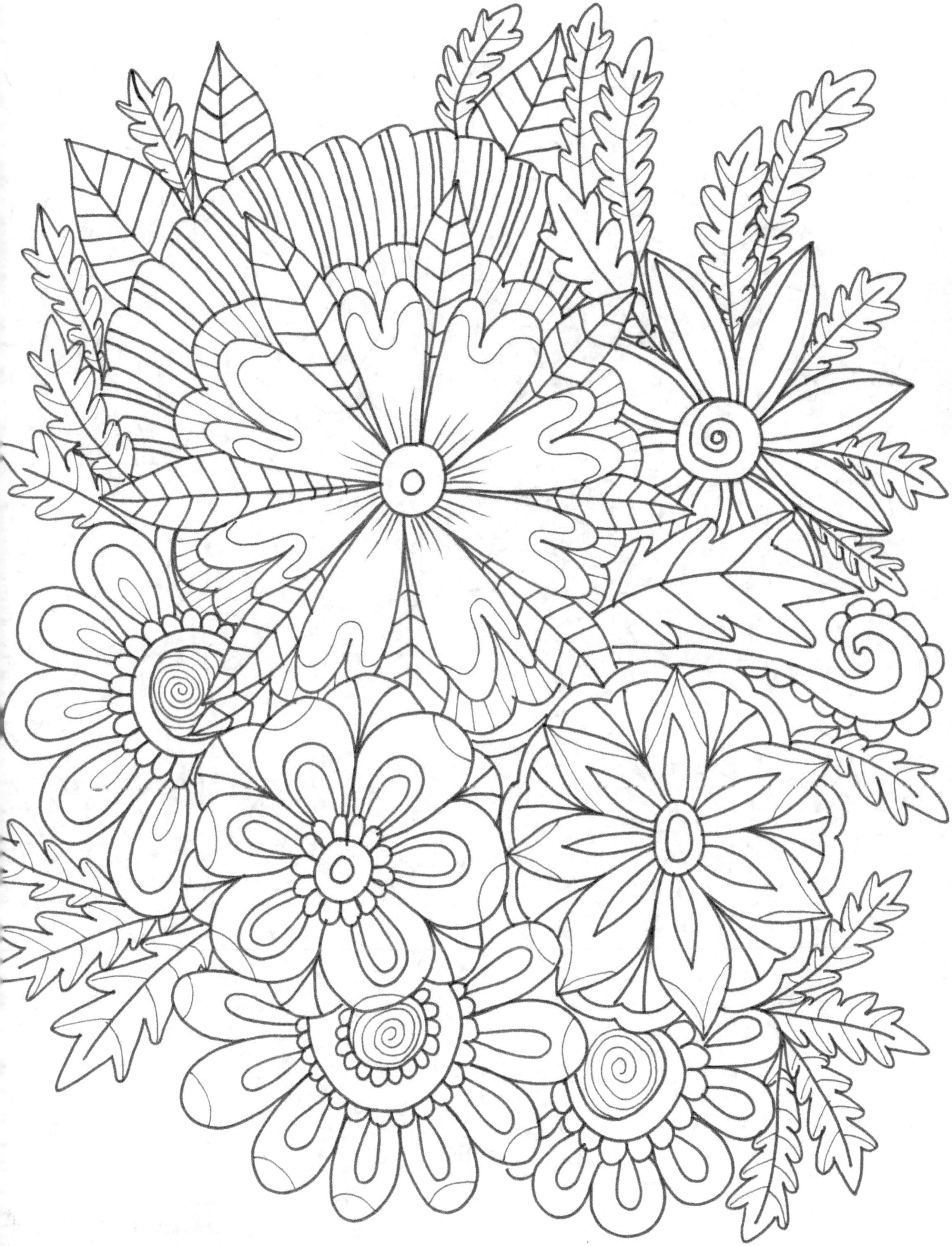

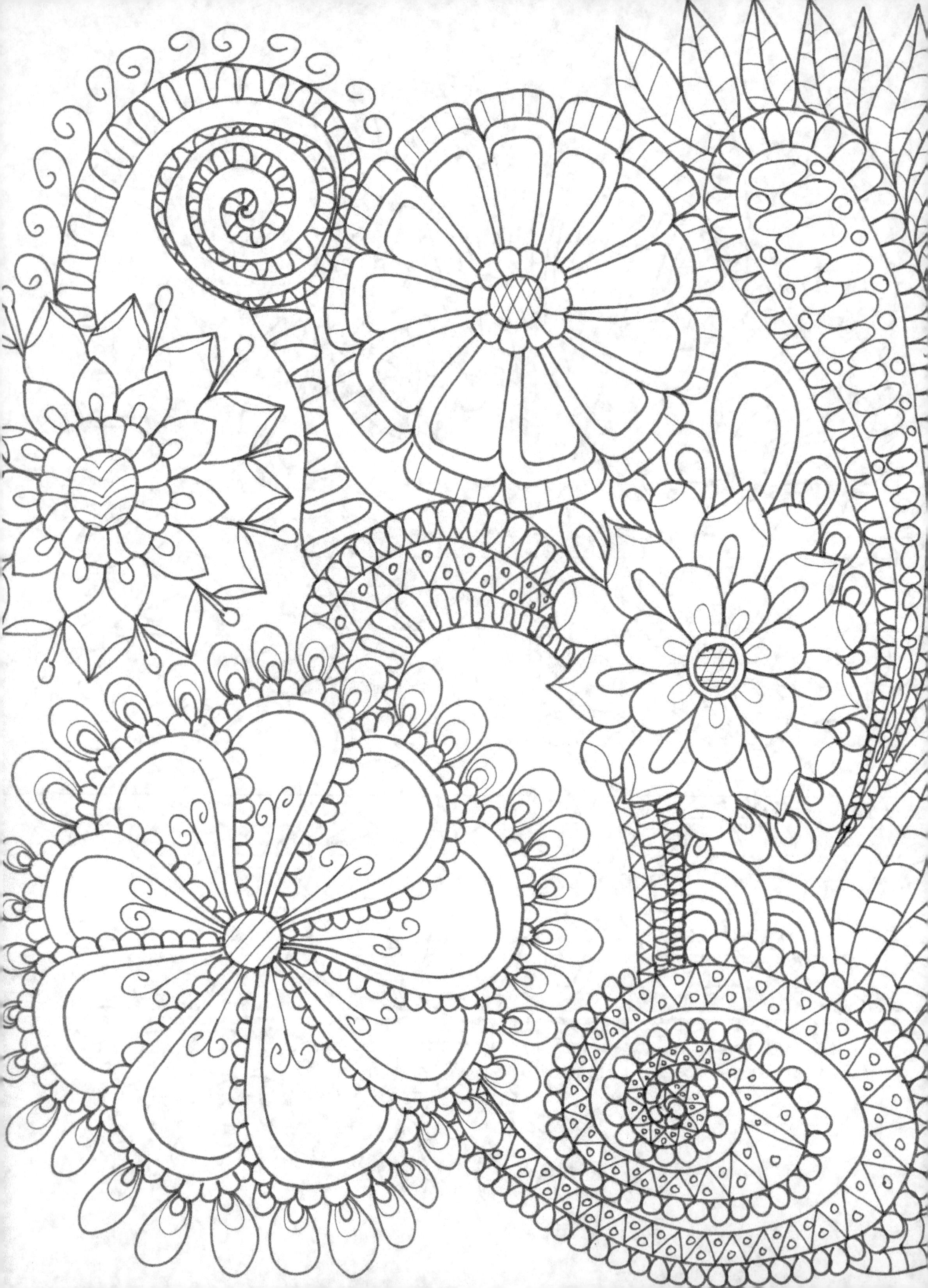

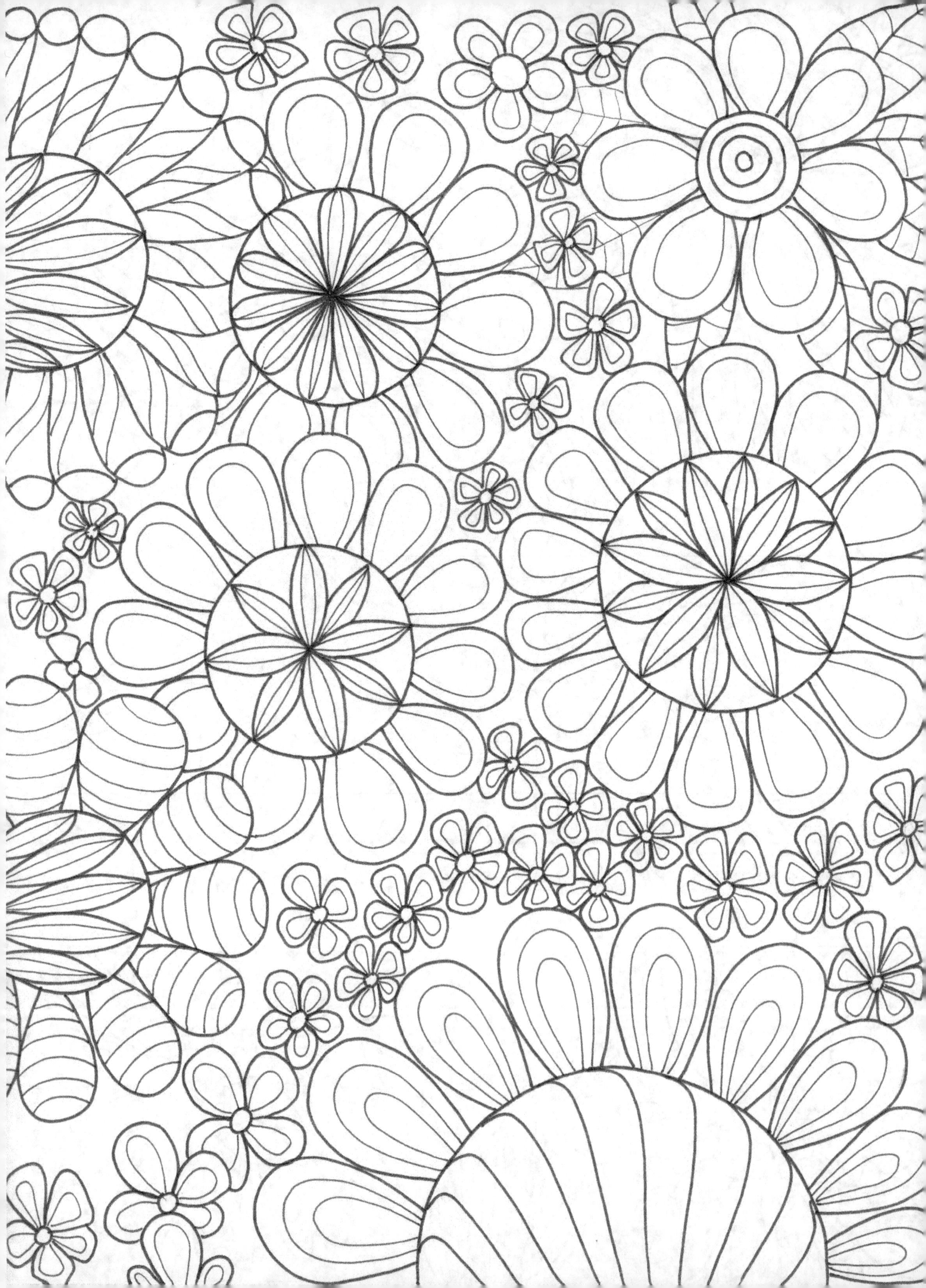

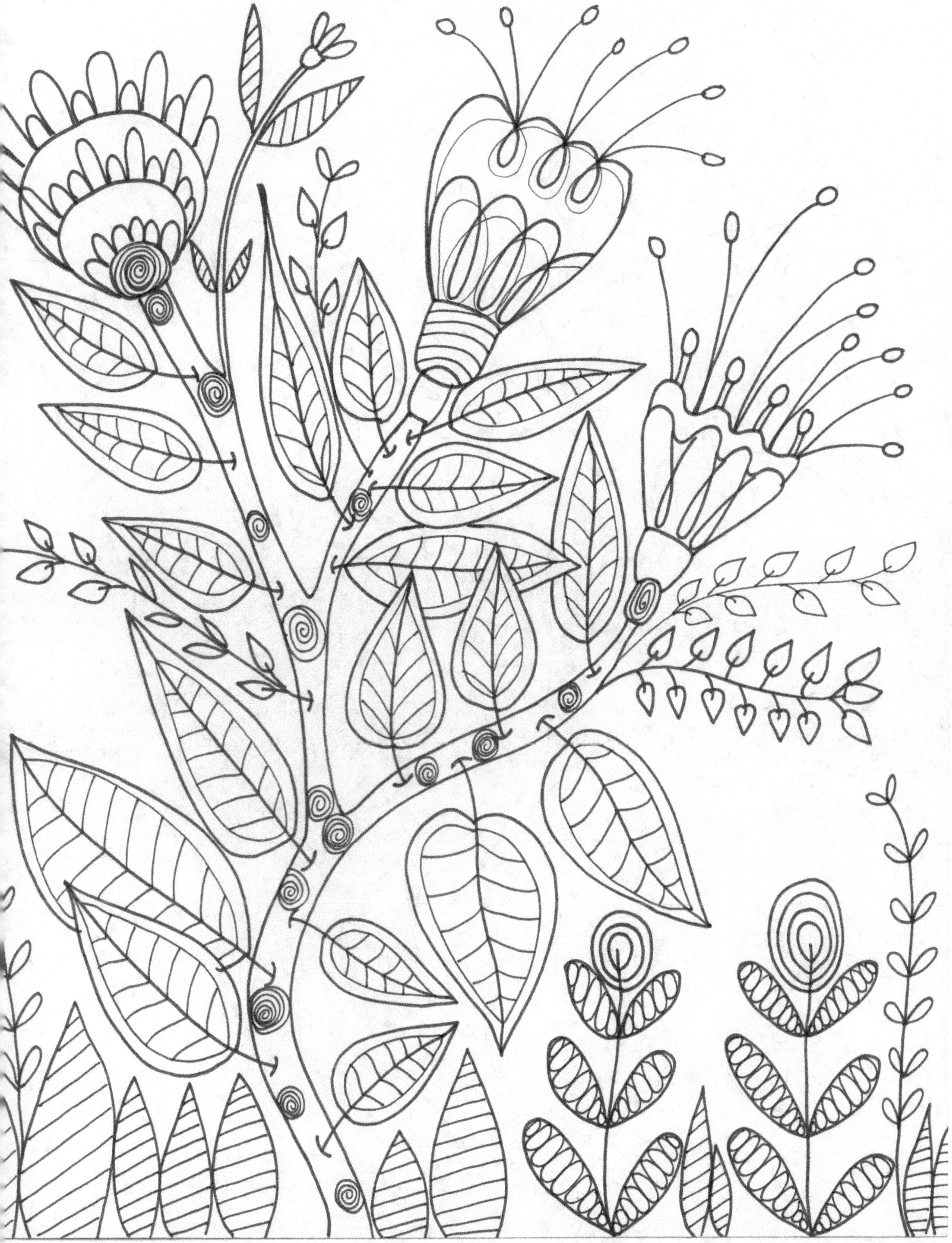

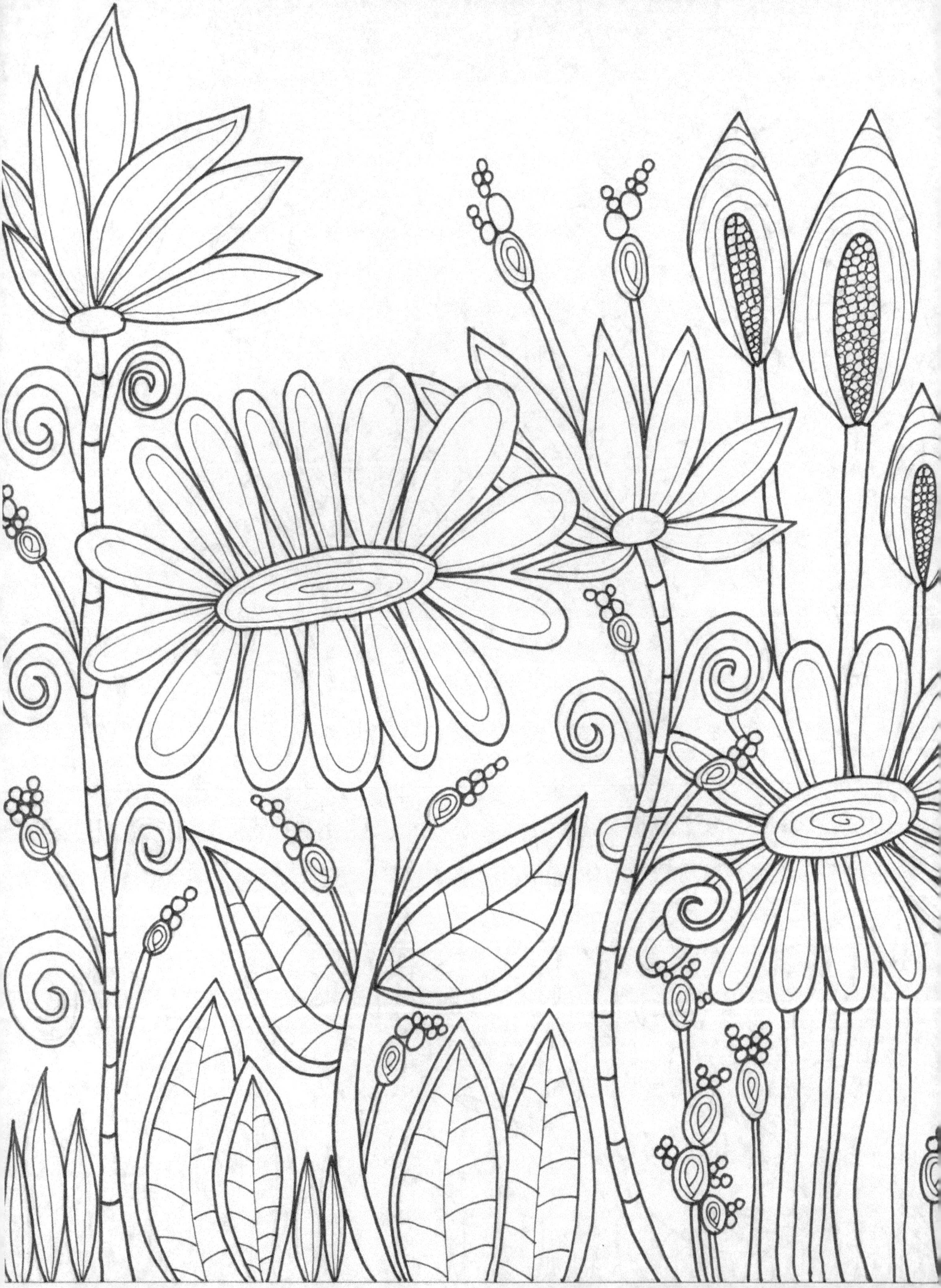

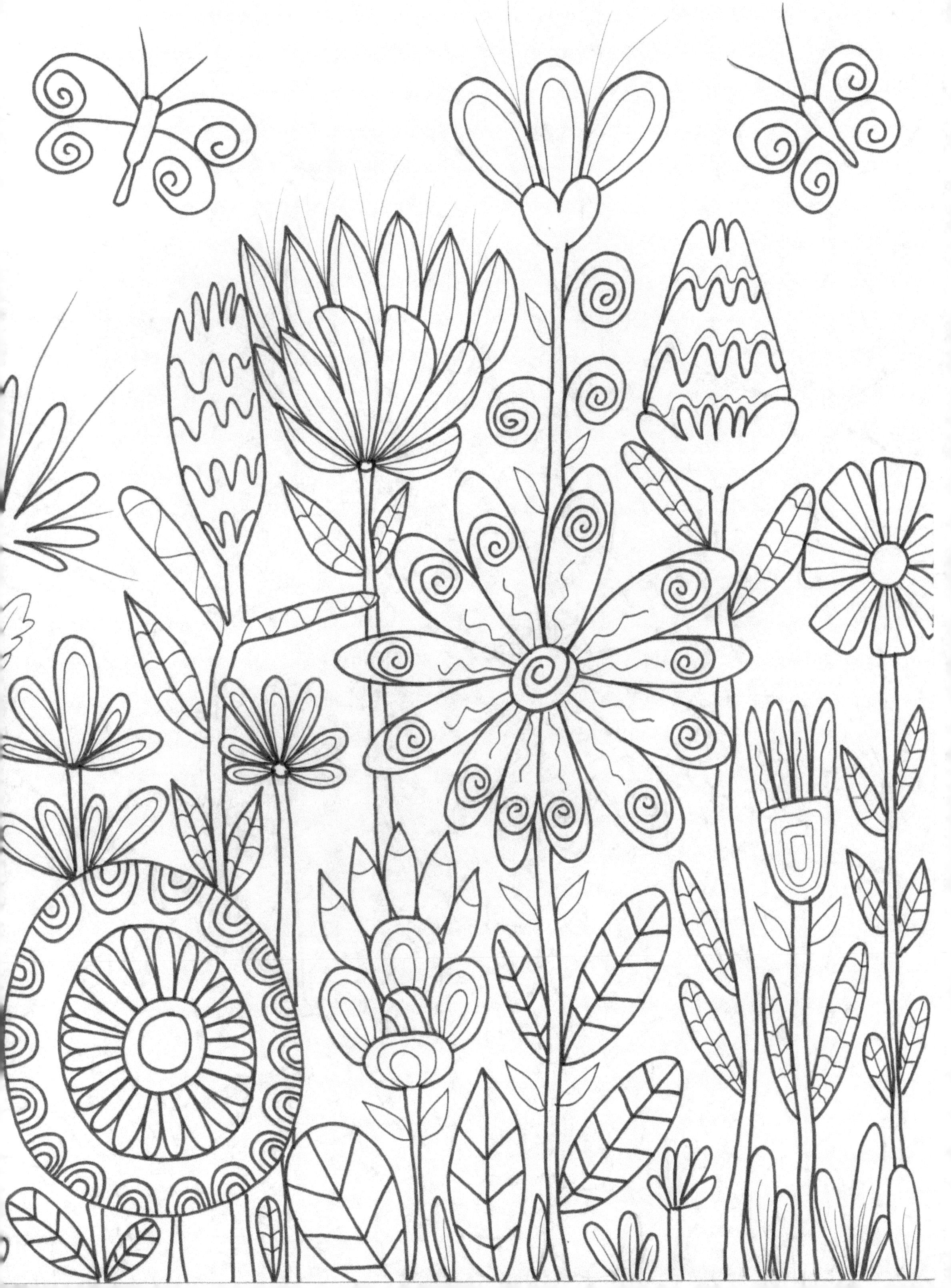

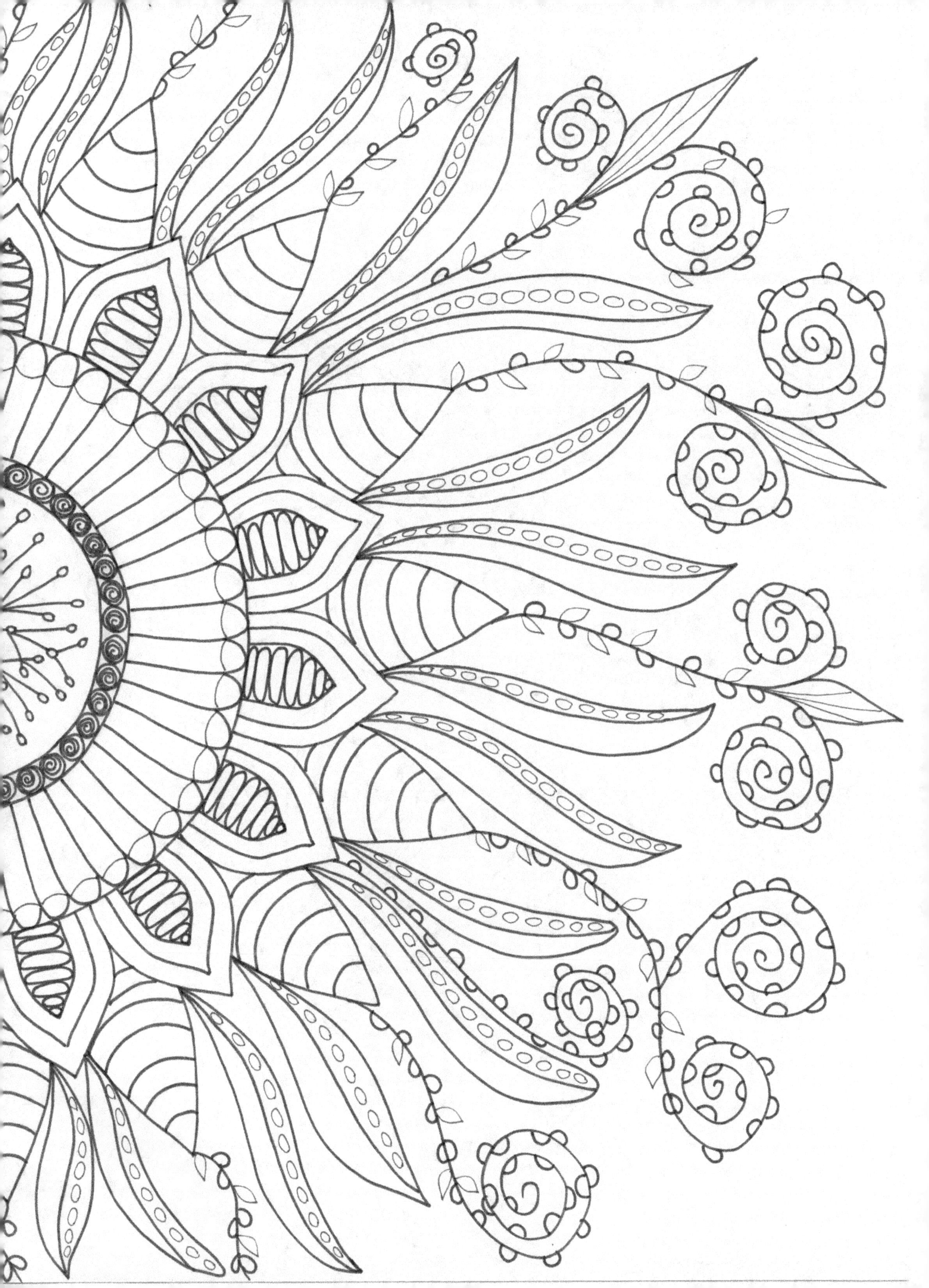

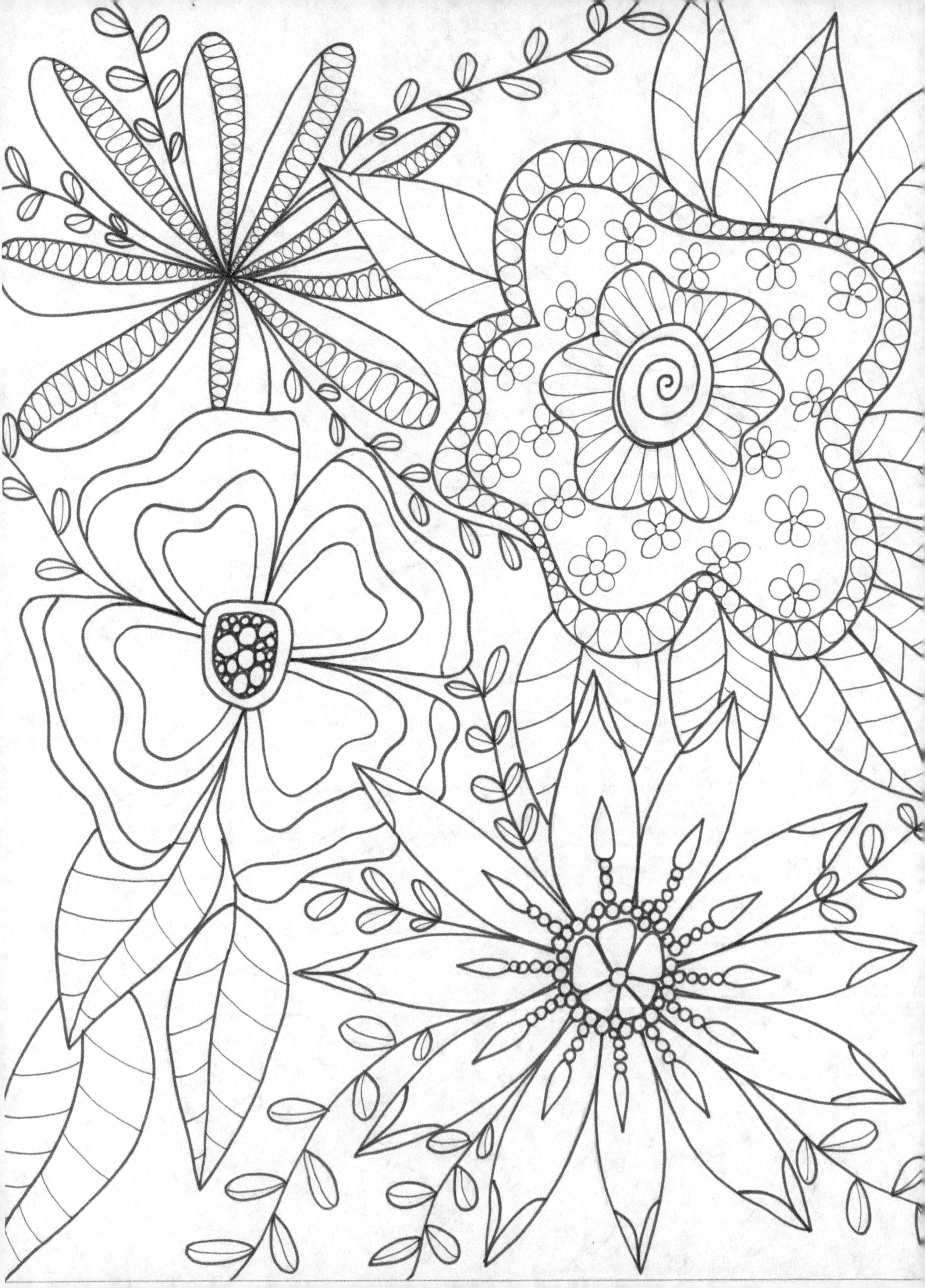

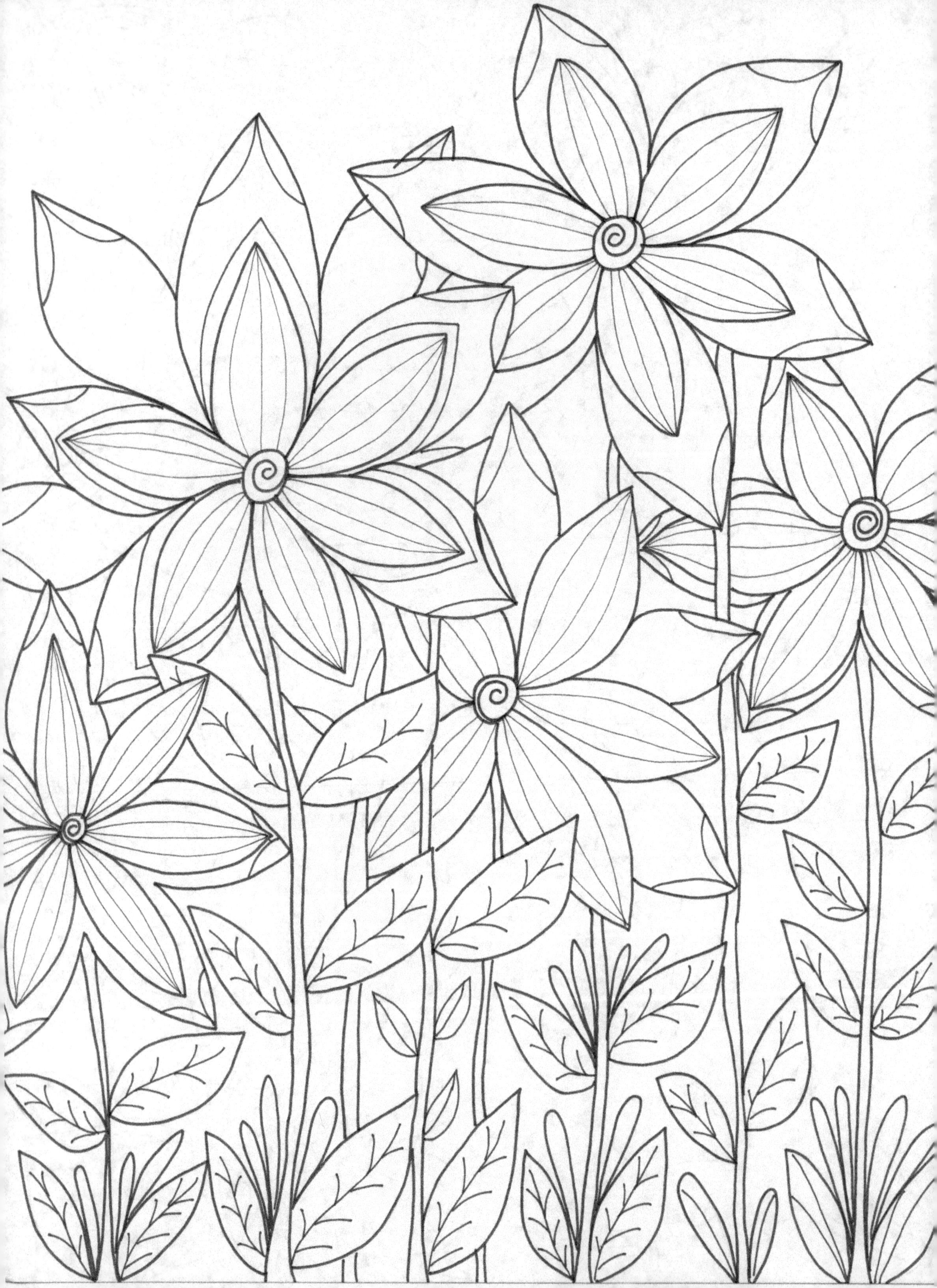

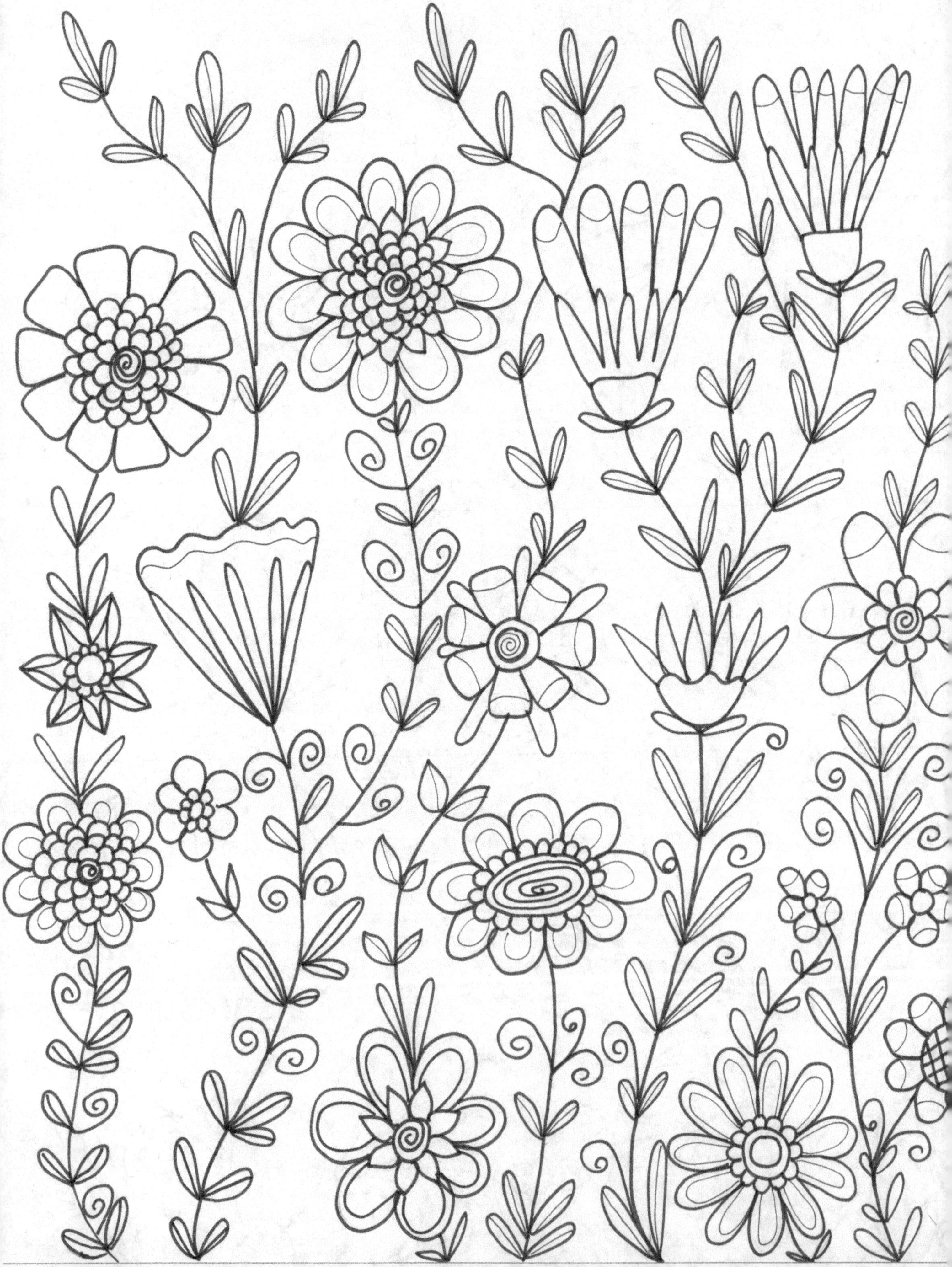

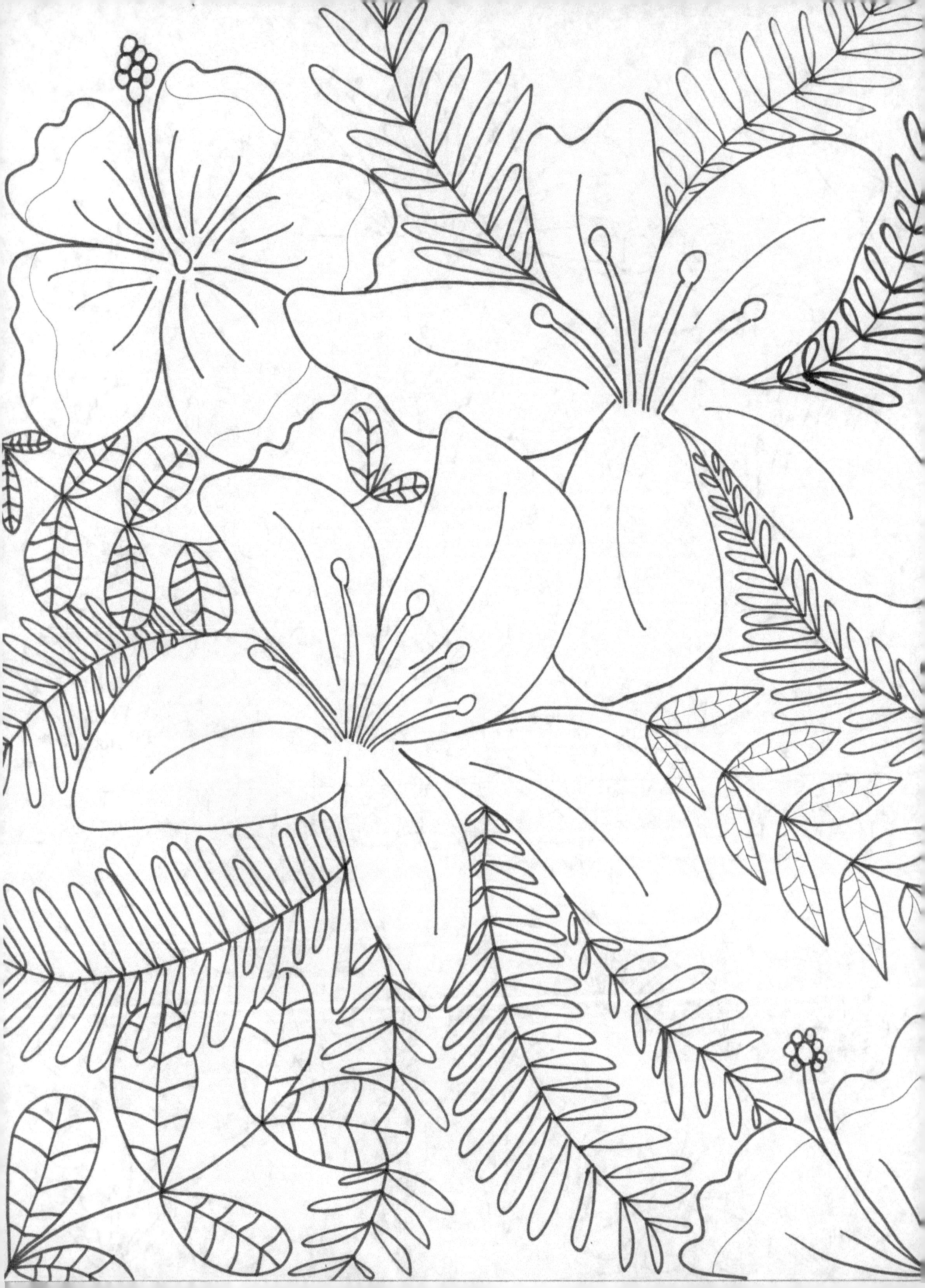

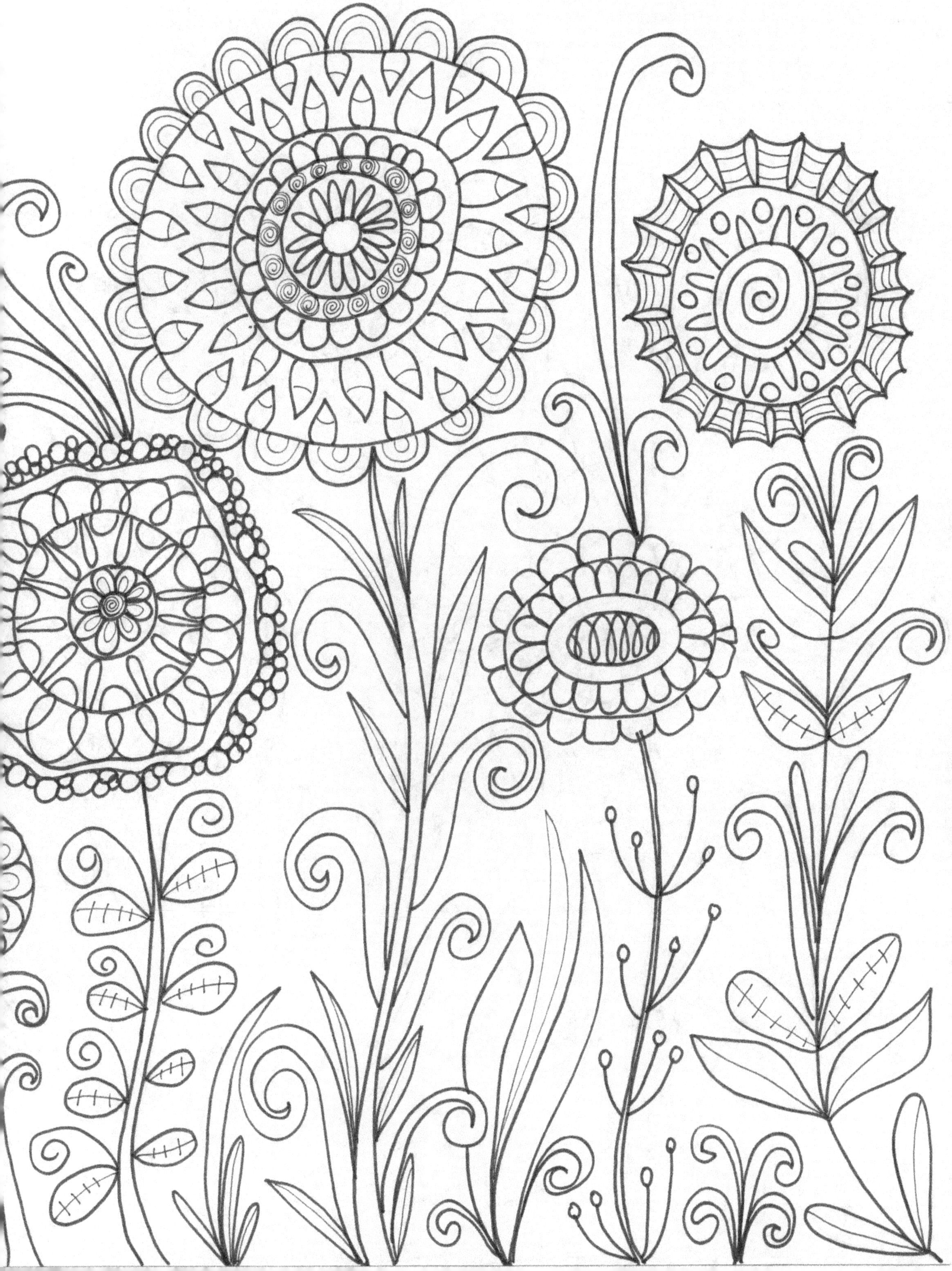

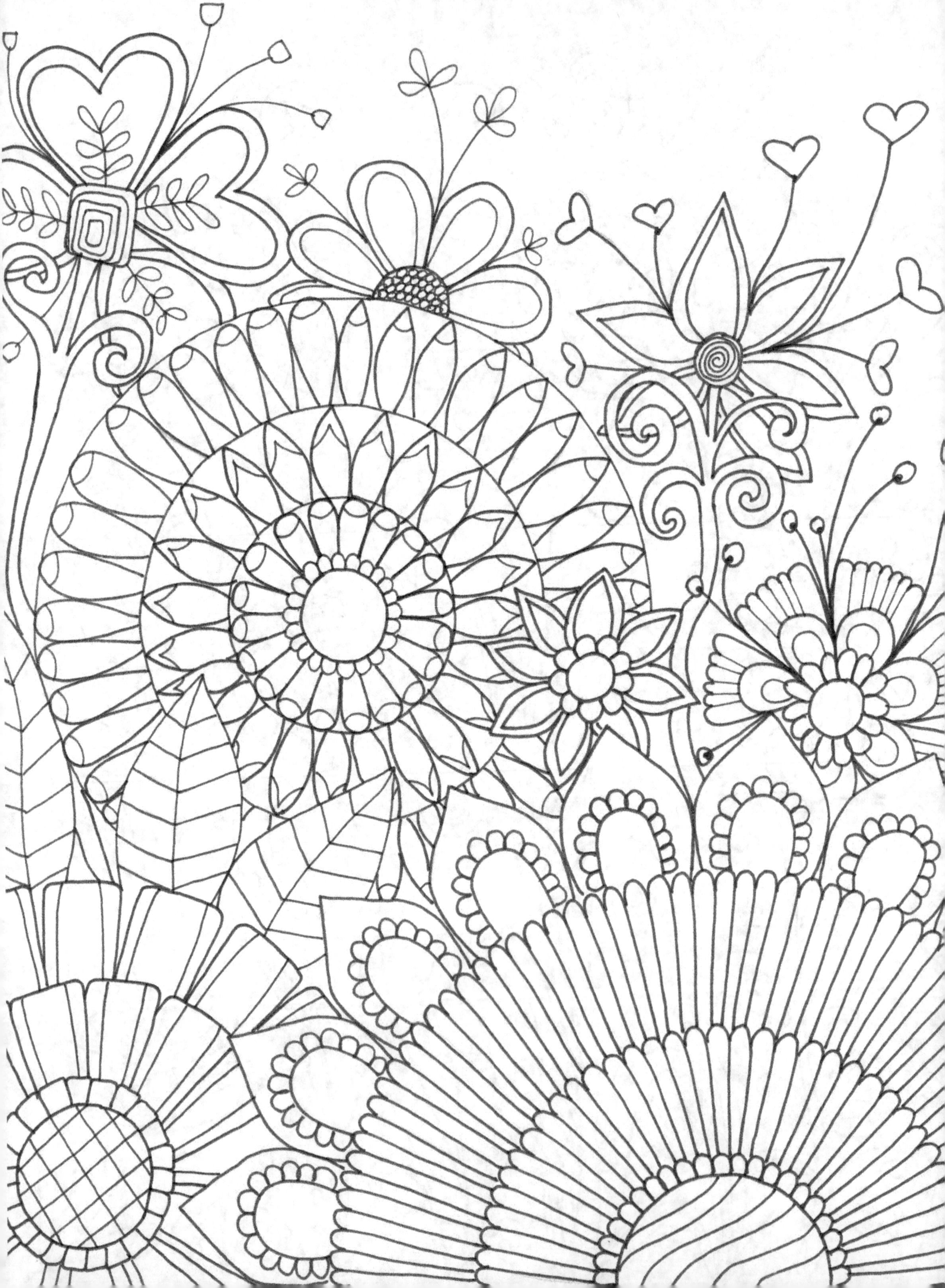

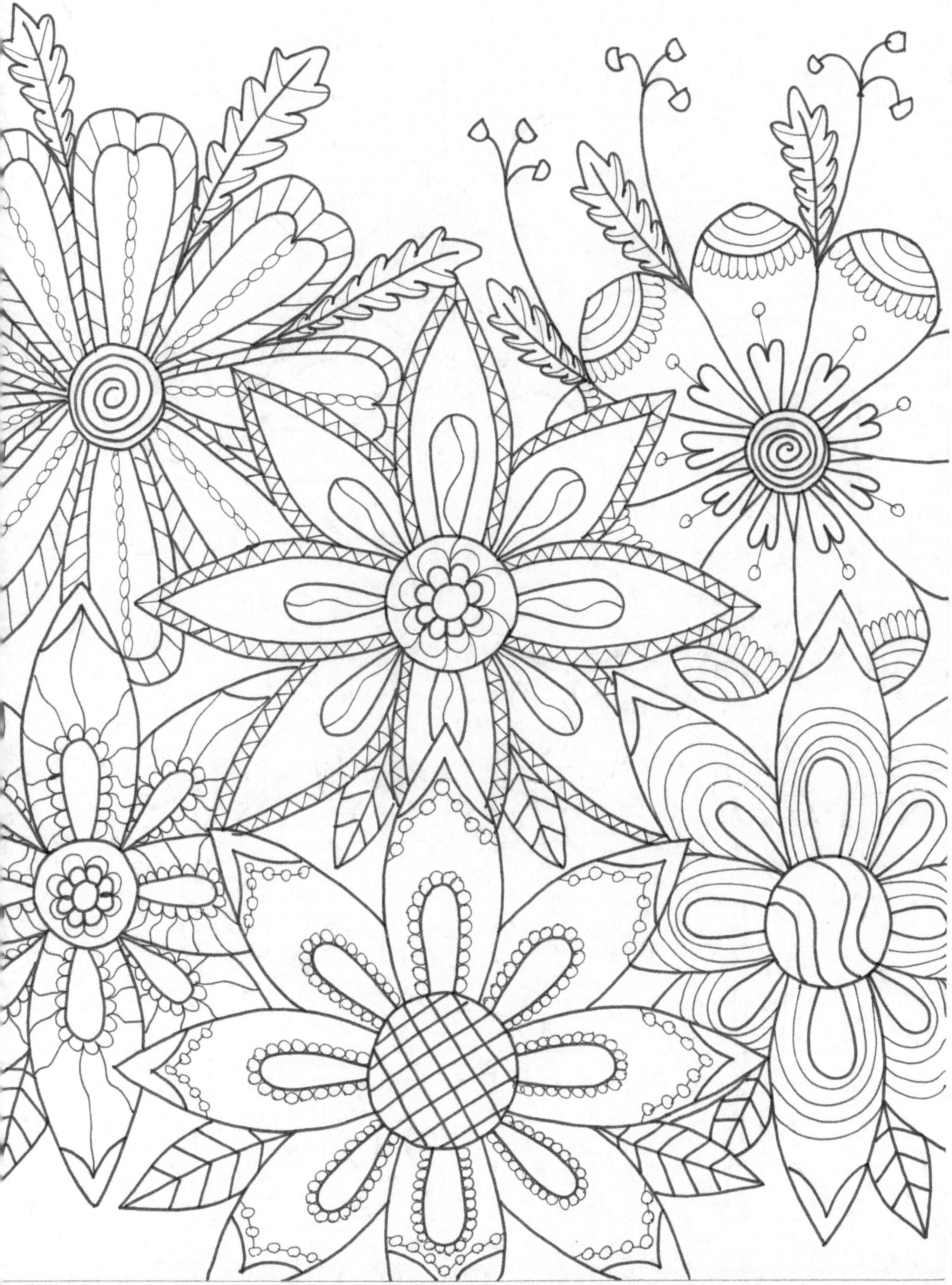

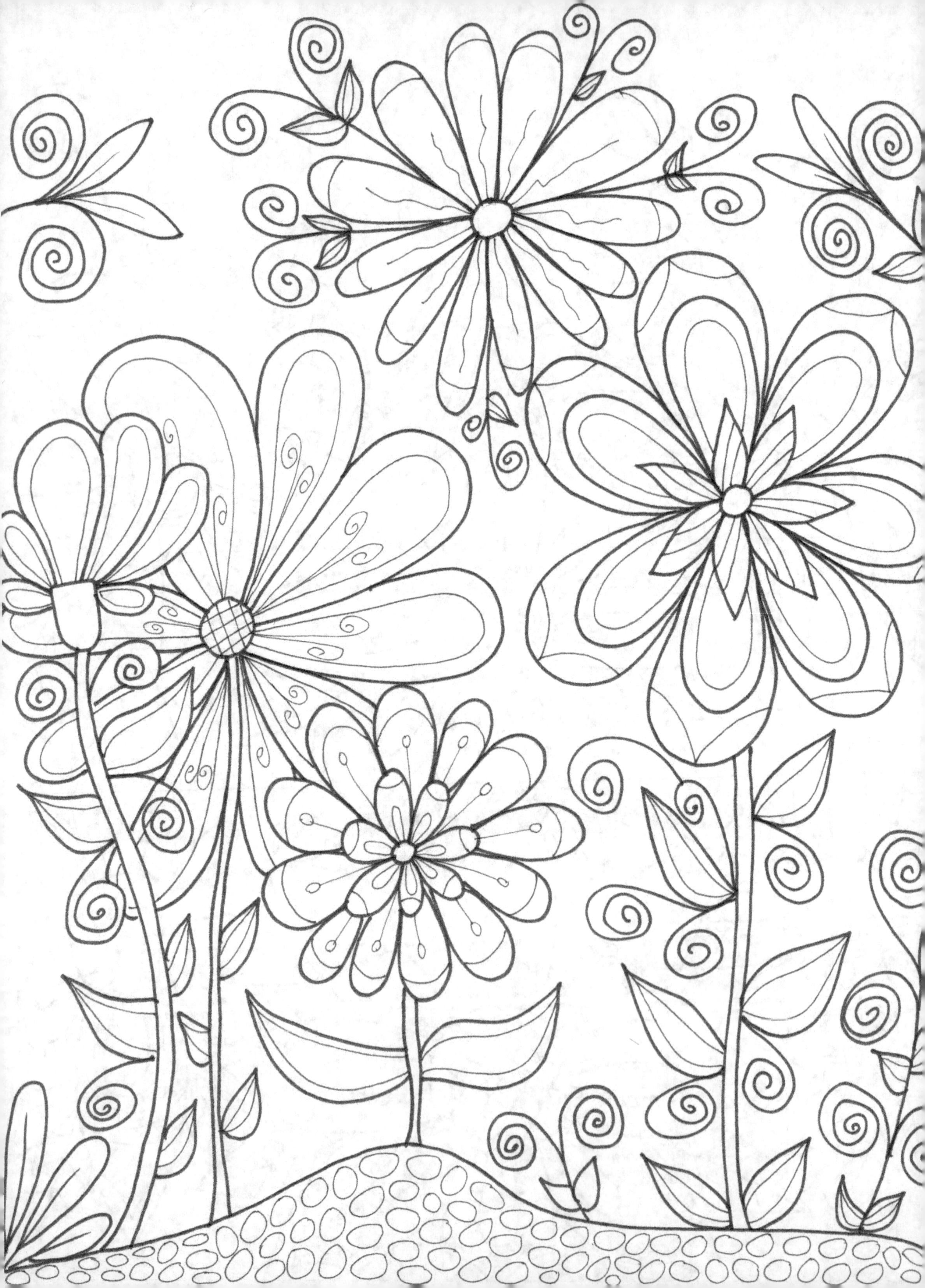

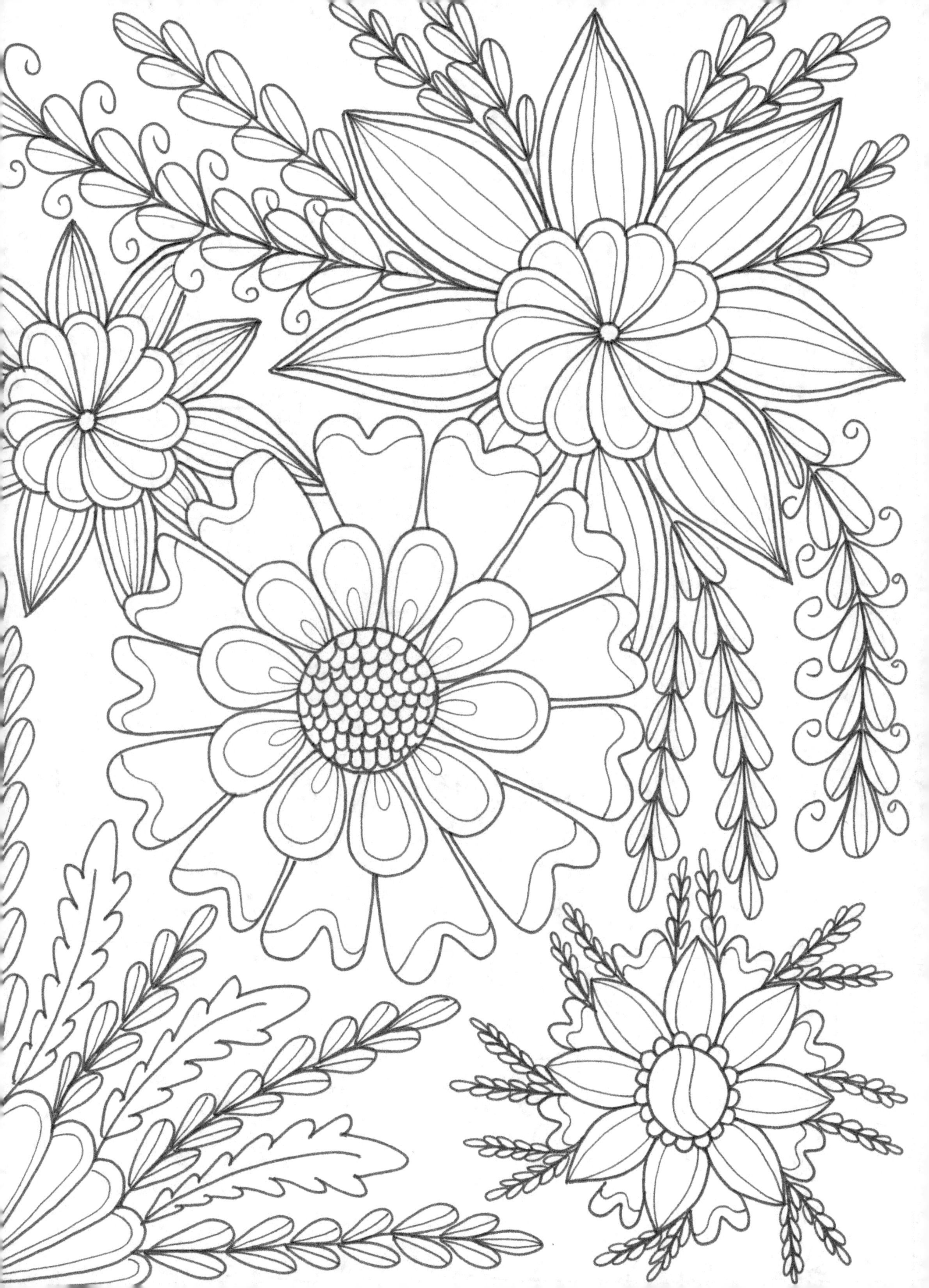

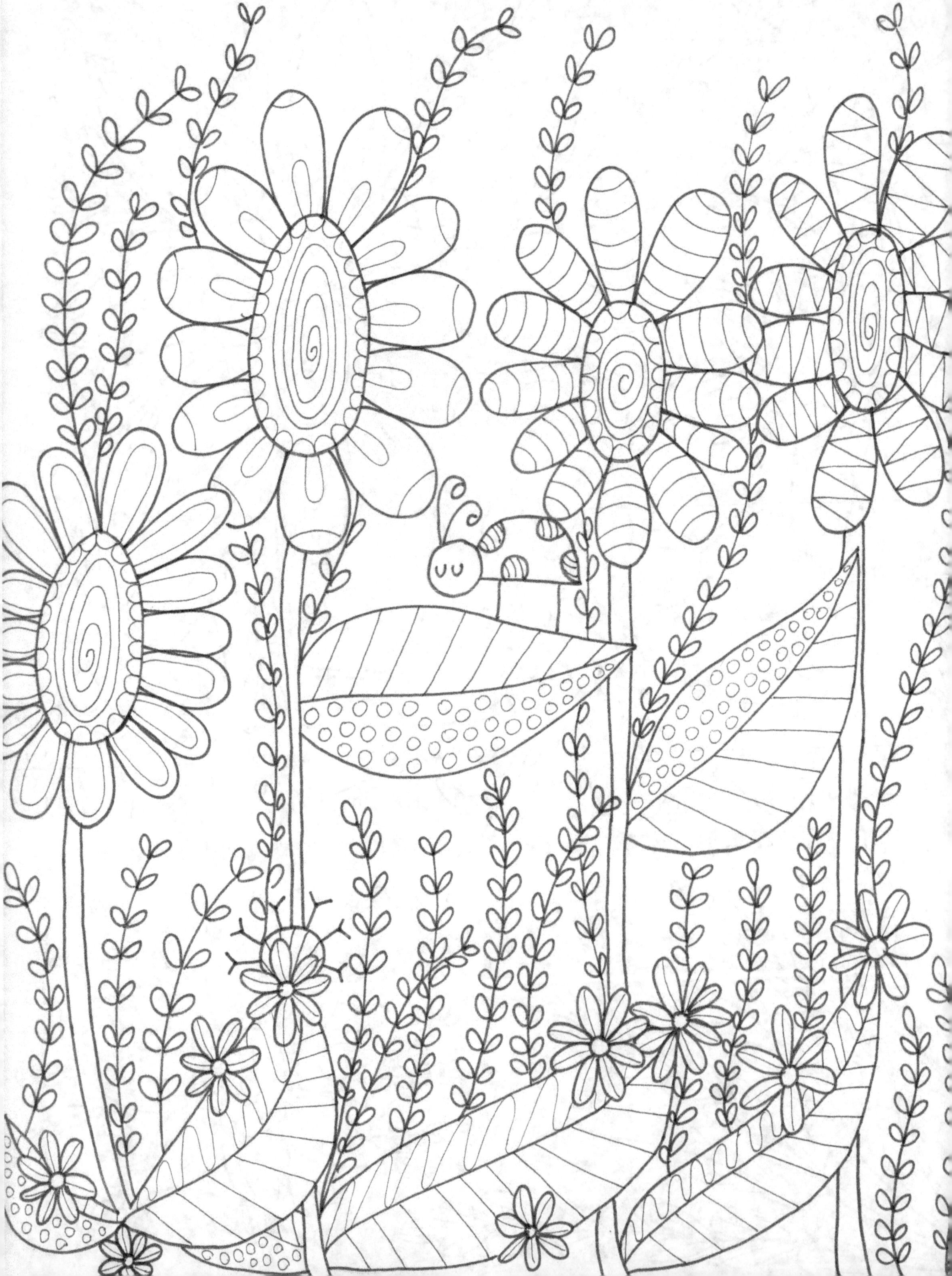

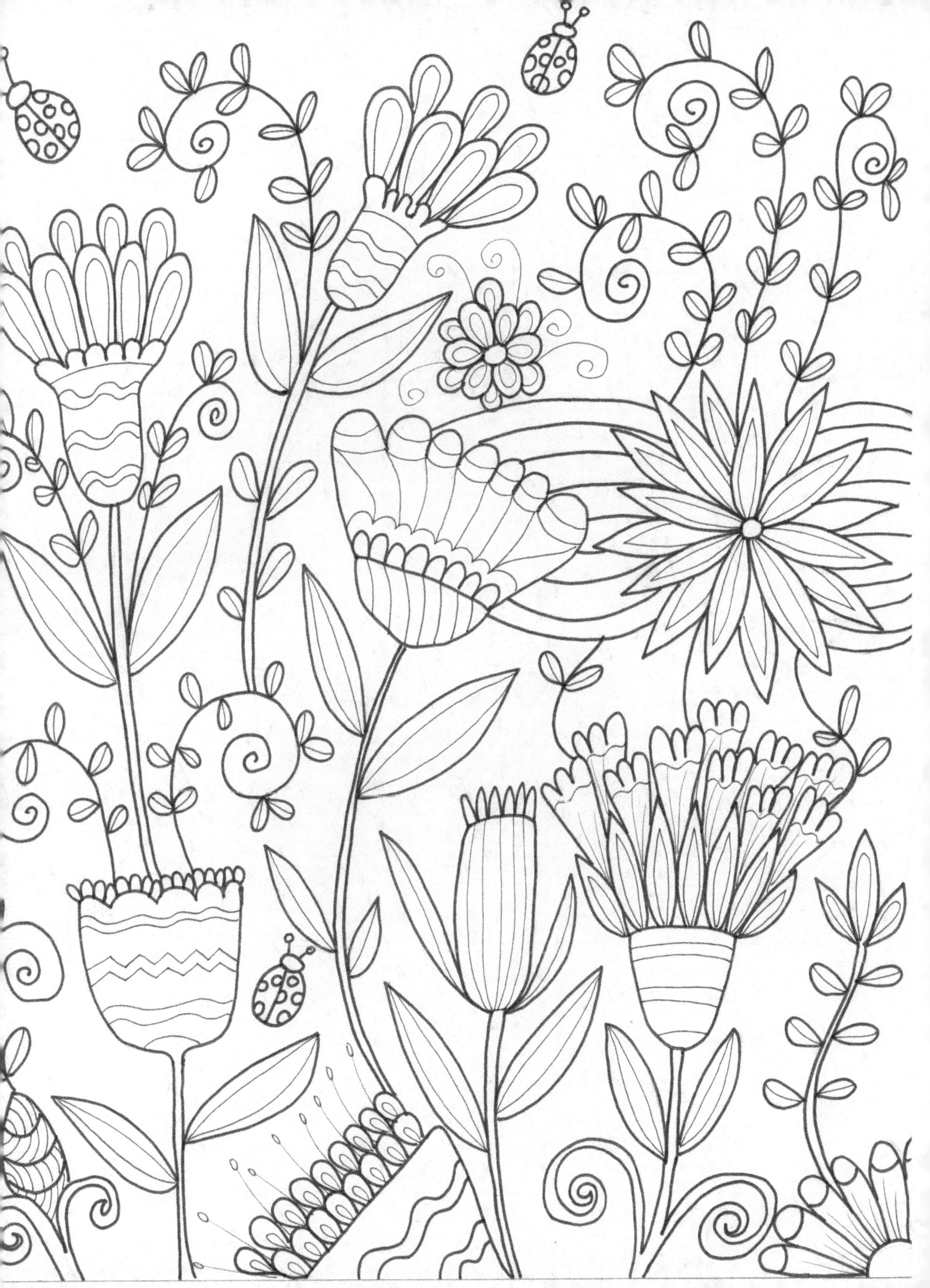

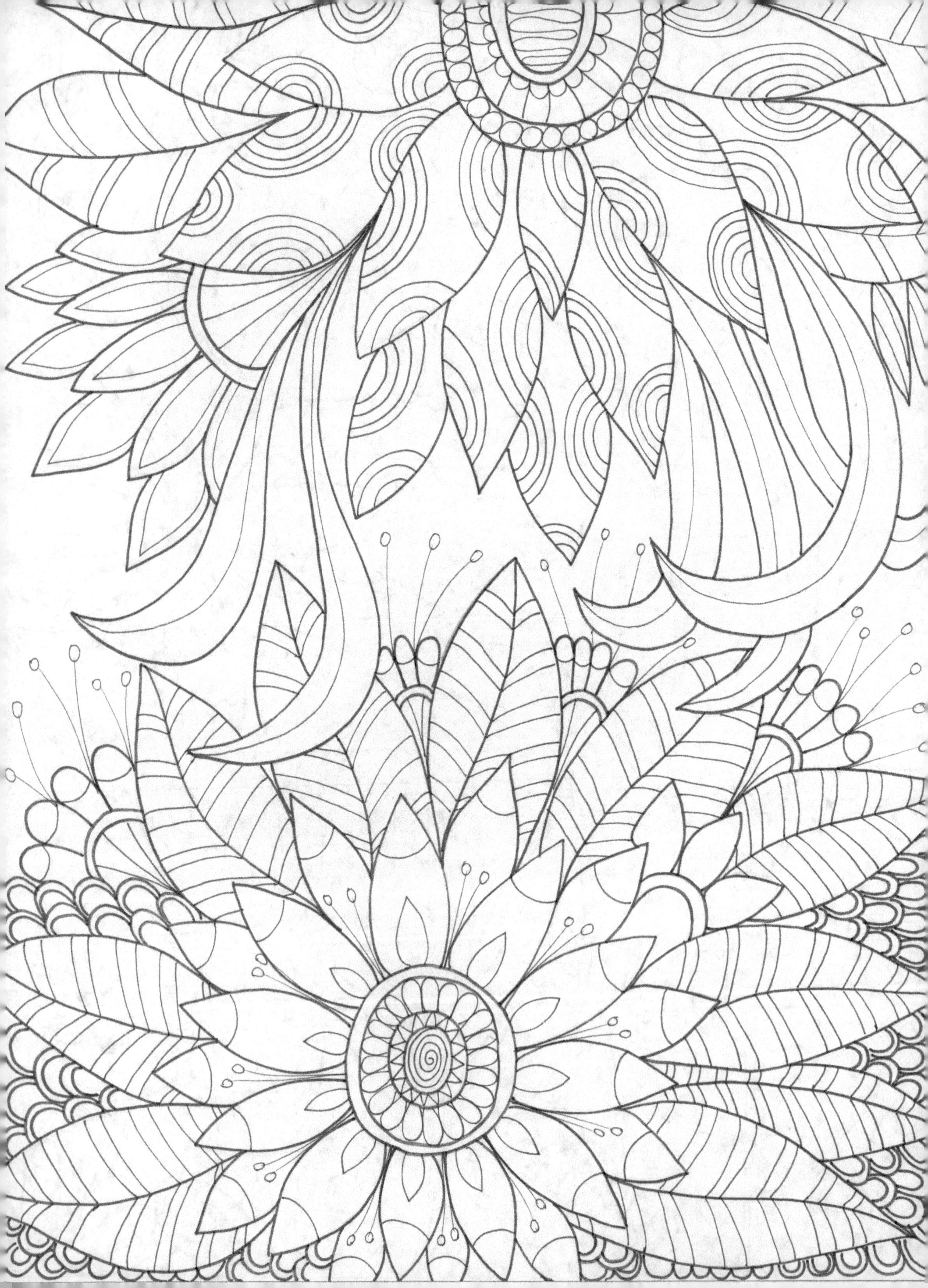

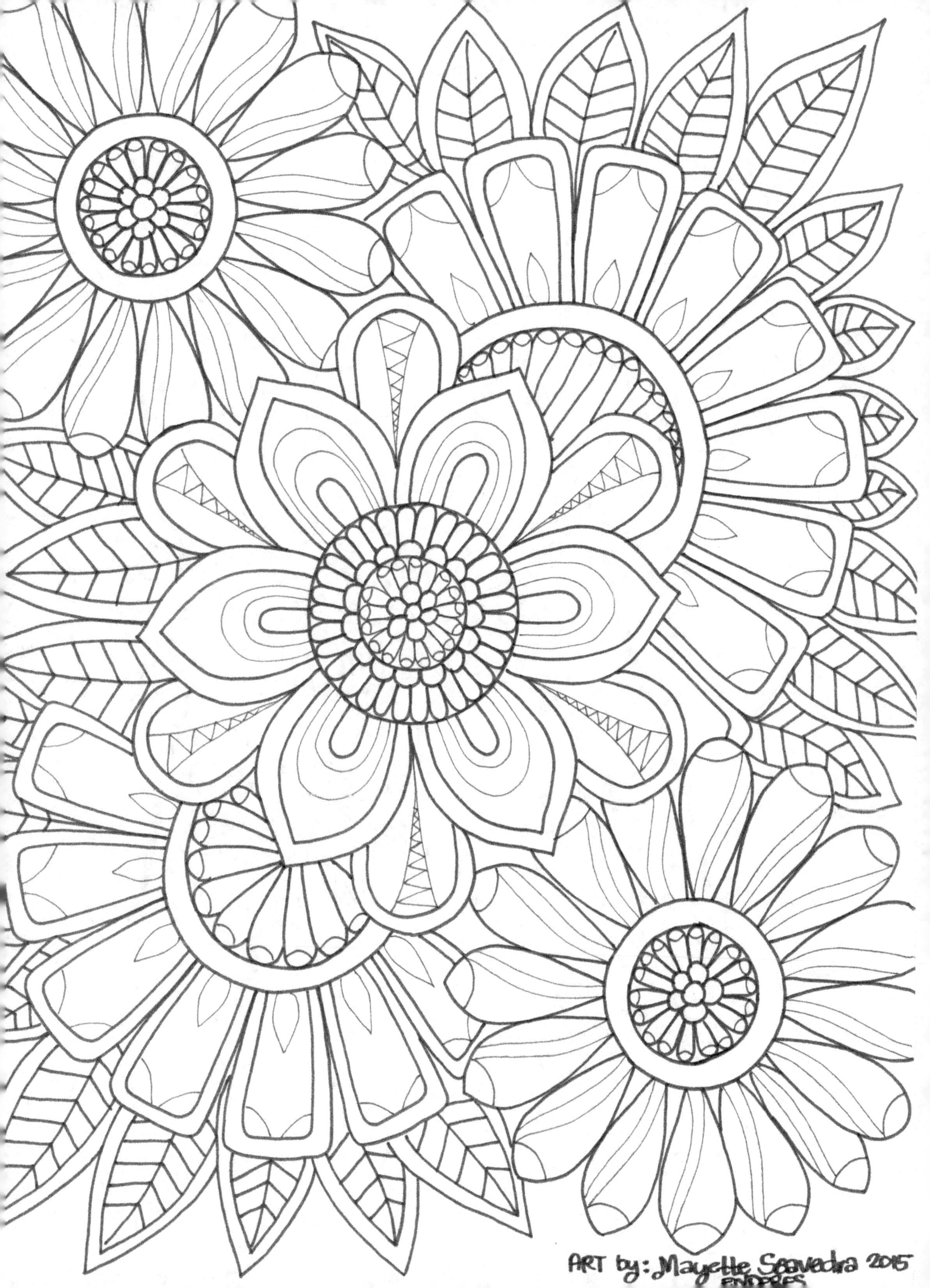
ART by: Mayette Saavedra 2015

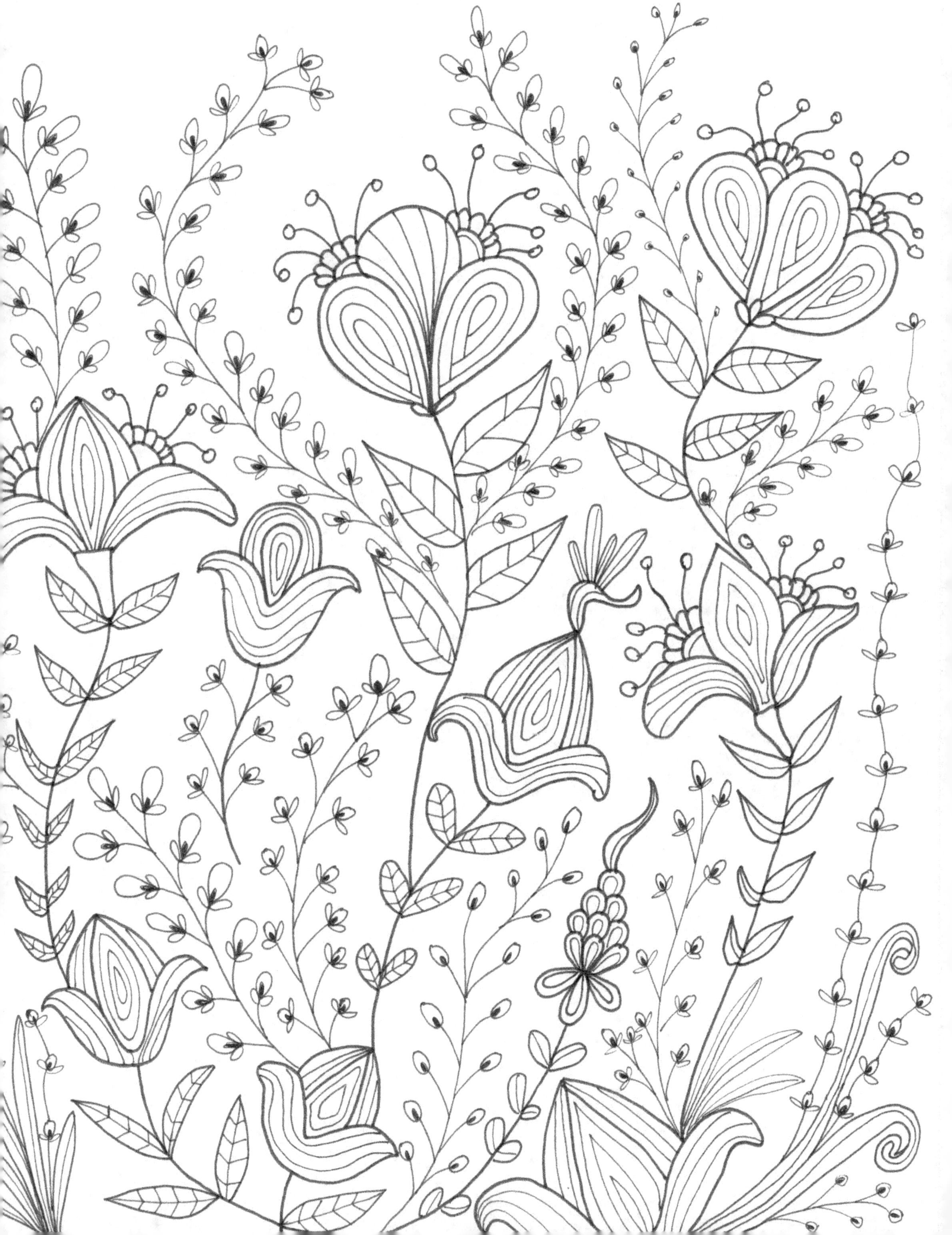

www.ingramcontent.com/pod-product-compliance
Lightning Source LLC
Chambersburg PA
CBHW081147170526
45158CB00009BA/2761
* 9 7 8 1 3 2 9 8 0 7 6 9 3 *